Adventure-filled Jokes for Children

LAUGH OUT LOUD

Hilarious Jokes for Happy Kids

Copyright-All Rights Reserved

This book has copyright protection. You can use the book for personal purpose. You should not see, use, alter, distribute, quote, take excerpts or paraphrase in part or whole the material contained in this book without obtaining the permission of the author first.

Introduction

Welcome to "Laugh Out Loud: A Joke Book for Kids"!

Get ready to embark on a sidesplitting journey filled with giggles, guffaws, and gut-busting hilarity! This book is your ticket to a world of laughter, where the silliest jokes and wittiest riddles await you.

Inside these pages, you'll discover a treasure trove of knee-slappers, puns, and clever one-liners that are sure to tickle your funny bone. Whether you're a seasoned jokester or just starting your comedic journey, there's something here for everyone.

From knock-knock jokes that'll leave you in stitches to animal-themed puns that'll have you roaring with laughter, "Laugh Out Loud" is the ultimate source of amusement for kids of all ages. Share these jokes with your friends, family, and even your pet hamster – because laughter knows no bounds!

Remember, a day without laughter is like a day without sunshine. So, let's dive into the wonderful world of jokes and create a symphony of laughter that'll echo through the corridors of your imagination.

Are you ready to laugh out loud? Then turn the page and let the chuckles begin!

Animal Jokes

1 What do you call a dinosaur that's sleeping?
A dino-snore!

2 How do you make a tissue dance?
You put a little boogie in it!

3 What do you get when you cross a snowman and a dog?
Frostbite!

4 Why don't elephants use computers?
Because they're afraid of the mouse!

5 Why did the crab never share?
Because he's shellfish!

6 How do you communicate with a fish?
You drop it a line!

7 Why don't skeletons fight each other?
They don't have the guts!

8 What do you call a bear with no teeth?
A gummy bear!

9 Why did the chicken join a band?
Because it had the drumsticks!

10 What do you get when you cross a sheep and a kangaroo?
A woolly jumper!

11 How do you catch a squirrel?
Climb a tree and act like a nut!

12 What do you call a happy pig?
A jolly good ham!

13 Why was the math book sad?
Because it had too many problems!

14 How does a lion greet the other animals in the field?
"Pleased to eat you!"

15 What's a frog's favorite candy?
Lollihops!

16 Why did the turtle refuse to play cards? Because it got tired of being dealt with!

17 What do you call a snobbish criminal going downstairs? A condescending con descending!

18 Why don't ants get sick? Because they have tiny ant-bodies!

19 How do you make a tissue dance? Put a little boogie in it!

20 Why don't some fish play piano? You can't tuna fish!

21 Why do bees have sticky hair?
Because they use honeycombs!

22 What do you call a bear with no teeth?
A gummy bear!

23 Why did the cow go to outer space?
To see the moooon!

24 How do you catch a squirrel?
Climb a tree and act like a nut!

25 What do you call a fish who wears a crown?
King Neptune!

26 Why don't elephants use computers?
Because they are afraid of the mouse!

27 What do you get when you cross a snake and a pie?
A python!

28 What do you call a happy cat?
A purr-son!

29 Why did the crab never share?
Because he's shellfish!

30 How do you organize a space party?
You planet!

31 Why did the elephant bring a suitcase to the zoo? Because it wanted to pack its trunk!

32 What do you call a bear with no ears? B!

33 How do you catch a squirrel with no legs? Unique, you wait for it to come to you!

34 What do you call a pig who knows karate? Pork chop!

35 Why did the chicken go to space? To visit the egg-stronauts!

36 How do you fix a broken tomato?
With tomato paste!

37 What's a tree's favorite drink?
Root beer!

38 Why don't ducks tell jokes while they're flying?
Because they might quack up!

39 What do you get when you cross a snake and a pie?
A python!

40 What do you call a monkey with a banana in each ear?
Anything you want, it can't hear you!

41 What do you call a dinosaur that's sleeping? A dino-snore!

42 What do you call a pig that does karate? A pork chop!

43 What did the buffalo say to his son when he left for school? Bison!

44 How do you keep a bull from charging? Take away its credit card!

45 What did one ocean say to the other ocean? Nothing, they just waved!

46 Why did the chicken join a band?
Because it had the drumsticks!

47 How do you catch a squirrel?
Climb a tree and act like a nut!

48 What do you call a happy pig?
A jolly good ham!

49 Why did the elephant bring a suitcase to the zoo?
Because it wanted to pack its trunk!

50 How do you communicate with a fish?
You drop it a line!

Food Jokes

1 What do you call cheese that isn't yours?
Nacho cheese!

2 Why did the tomato turn red?
Because it saw the salad dressing!

3 How do you fix a broken tomato?
With tomato paste!

4 Why don't eggs tell jokes?
Because they might crack up!

5 What did the lettuce say to the celery?
Let's be friends, we make a great salad together!

6 Why did the cookie go to the doctor?
Because it was feeling crumby!

7 What do you call a fake noodle?
An impasta!

8 Why don't some vegetables like to play cards?
Because they might get beet!

9 What do you call a sleeping pizza?
PizzzZzzza!

10 Why did the orange stop in the middle of the road?
Because it ran out of juice!

11 What did one plate say to the other plate?
Tonight, dinner's on me!

12 Why did the banana go to the party?
Because it was a-peeling!

13 How do you make a lemon drop?
Just let it fall!

14 What do you call a peanut in a spacesuit?
An astronut!

15 Why did the vegetable go to the art gallery?
To turnip its nose at the paintings!

16 What do you get when you cross a snowman and a vampire?
Frostbite!

17 What's a skeleton's favorite vegetable?
Spare ribs!

18 Why did the gum cross the road?
Because it was stuck to the chicken's foot!

19 How do you organize a space party?
You planet!

20 What kind of fruit do trees like the most?
Pineapples!

21 Why did the scarecrow win an award?
Because he was outstanding in his field!

22 Why did the gingerbread man go to school?
To improve his "cookie-culation"!

23 What's the difference between a chef and a chemist?
A chef cooks and a chemist makes everything cook!

24 Why was the little strawberry crying?
Because its parents were in a jam!

25 What do you call a dinosaur with an extensive vocabulary?
A thesaurus!

26 What did the hamburger name its baby?
Patty!

27 How do you make a watermelon smile?
You water it!

28 Why did the girl bring a ladder to the bar?
Because she heard the drinks were on the house!

29 Why don't eggs ever tell jokes?
Because they might crack up!

30 What do you call two bananas?
A pair of slippers!

31 Why did the kid bring a ladder to school?
Because it was high school!

32 How do you catch a squirrel with no legs?
Unique, you wait for it to come to you!

33 Why do hamburgers go to the gym?
To get their buns in shape!

34 Why did the cookie cry?
Because its mother was a wafer too long!

35 What do you get if you cross a snowman and a dog?
Frostbite!

36 How do you make a milkshake?
Give it a good scare!

37 Why don't skeletons fight each other?
They don't have the guts!

38 What did one pancake say to the other pancake at the breakfast table?
"Time to flip out!"

39 What's a pizza's favorite song?
"Slice, Slice Baby!"

40 Why did the tomato go out with a prune?
Because it couldn't find a date!

41 How do you make an apple turnover?
Push it down a hill!

42 What do you call a fake noodle?
An impasta!

43 What did the salad say to the lettuce at the party?
Lettuce romaine friends!

44 Why did the grape stop in the middle of the road?
Because it ran out of juice!

45 What's orange and sounds like a parrot?
A carrot!

46 How do you fix a cracked pumpkin?
With a pumpkin patch!

47 Why did the sandwich go to school?
Because it wanted to be a little "brrrrr-illiant"!

48 Why was the apple so lonely?
Because the oranges were all in a "peelings" contest!

49 Why did the lemon go to school?
Because it wanted to be a little "zest-ucated"!

50 Why were the cherries blushing?
Because they saw the banana split!

School Jokes

1 Why did the math book look sad?
Because it had too many problems!

2 Why did the teacher wear sunglasses to school?
Because her students were so bright!

3 Why did the pencil get a detention?
Because it couldn't stop drawing attention!

4 Why did the student eat their homework?
Because the teacher said it was a piece of cake!

5 Why did the music teacher go to jail?
Because she got caught with too many sharps and flats!

6 Why was the science book funny?
Because it had a lot of good jokes in its elements!

7 Why was the calendar always happy?
Because it had too many dates!

8 Why did the school take away the time-traveling class?
The students were always late!

9 Why did the geometry book go on a diet?
To lose some weight in its angles!

10 Why did the student wear glasses in the art class?
To improve their "i" sight!

11 What do librarians take with them when they go fishing?
Bookworms!

12 Why did the history book get sad when it lost a chapter?
It felt like it lost its past!

13 Why did the scarecrow win an award at school?
Because it was outstanding in its field!

14 Why do fish always know how much they weigh?
Because they have their own scales!

15 Why was the math book sad?
Because it had too many "problems"!

16 Why did the computer go to school?
To become smarter, byte by byte!

17 Why did the teacher wear sunglasses in class?
Because her students were so bright!

18 What did the zero say to the eight?
Nice belt!

19 Why was the math book sad?
Because it had too many problems.

20 Why did the scarecrow win an award?
Because he was outstanding in his field!

21 Why did the student wear glasses in the math class?
To improve division!

22 Why did the teacher go to the beach?
To test the waters!

23 What do you get when you cross a snowman and a vampire?
Frostbite!

24 Why do birds fly south for the winter?
Because it's too far to walk!

25 Why was the broom late to school?
It overswept!

26 What did the pencil sharpener say to the pencil?
Stop going in circles and get to the point!

27 Why did the tomato turn red?
Because it saw the salad dressing!

28 What did the ruler say to the pencil?
I'll always be your straight edge!

29 What do you call a piece of paper that likes to be funny?
A laugh-ter!

30 Why was the letter A so cool in class?
Because it sat next to the fan!

31 Why did the kid bring a ladder to school?
Because it was high school!

32 Why did the teacher go to the beach?
To test the waters!

33 What is a teacher's favorite nation?
Expla-nation!

34 Why did the boy bring a ladder to school?
Because he wanted to go to high school!

35 Why do magicians do well in school?
They're great at trick questions!

36 Why do fish live in saltwater?
Because pepper makes them sneeze!

37 What's the best tool to use in math class?
Multi-pliers!

38 Why was the computer cold?
It left its Windows open!

39 What do you call a notebook that tells jokes?
A laugh book!

40 Why did the tomato turn red?
Because it saw the salad dressing!

41 Why did the student wear glasses in the math class? To improve division!

42 What did the little math book say to the big math book? "I've got a lot of problems!"

43 Why did the teacher go to the beach? To test the waters!

44 What do you call a piece of paper that likes to be funny? A laugh-ter!

45 Why was the letter A so cool in class? Because it sat next to the fan!

46 Why did the kid bring a ladder to school? Because it was high school!

47 Why did the teacher go to the beach? To test the waters!

48 What is a teacher's favorite nation? Expla-nation!

49 Why did the boy bring a ladder to school? Because he wanted to go to high school!

50 Why do magicians do well in school? They're great at trick questions!

Doctor Jokes

1 Why did the doctor carry a red pen?
In case they needed to draw blood!

2 Why was the doctor always calm?
Because they had plenty of patients!

3 Why did the skeleton go to the doctor?
Because it was feeling a bit bonely!

4 Why did the skeleton go to the doctor?
Because it was feeling a bit bonely!

5 Why did the nurse always carry a red pen?
To draw blood!

6 Why did the doctor go to art school?
To learn how to draw blood!

7 Why did the doctor go to school?
To improve their patients' health!

8 Why did the doctor break up with their stethoscope?
It wasn't giving them enough heartbeats!

9 Why did the nurse bring a ladder to work?
To check up on their patients' height!

10 What did the doctor prescribe for a sick teddy bear?
Plenty of "teddycillin"!

11 Why did the doctor carry a pencil and paper to work?
To write "pain-staking" notes!

12 Why did the doctor go to the circus?
To check up on the clown's funny bone!

13 Why did the nurse bring a red pen to work?
To draw patients' blood... or maybe just doodle!

14 Why did the skeleton go to the doctor's office?
To get their "bone density" checked!

15 Why did the doctor bring a violin to the hospital?
To see if music could heal broken hearts!

16 What do you call a doctor who's also an artist? A "master of medicine"!

17 Why did the doctor take up gardening? To learn about plant "medicines"!

18 Why did the doctor become a chef? To learn how to "diagnose" the perfect recipe!

19 Why did the nurse become a teacher? To help patients learn about health and wellness!

20 Why did the doctor become a musician? To learn how to "tune" into their patients' needs!

21 Why did the nurse become a comedian?
To bring laughter and smiles to patients' faces!

22 Why did the doctor start a dance class?
To teach patients about the importance of movement!

23 Why did the nurse start a cooking show?
To share healthy recipes for patients to enjoy!

24 Why did the doctor become a detective?
To solve medical mysteries and help patients!

25 Why did the nurse become an author?
To write stories that inspire health and healing!

26 Why did the doctor go on a diet?
To set a healthy example for their patients!

27 Why did the nurse bring a clown to work?
To lift patients' spirits with laughter!

28 Why did the doctor become an inventor?
To create medical tools and devices for patients!

29 Why did the nurse become a coach?
To motivate patients to reach their health goals!

30 Why did the doctor become a magician?
To perform "medical miracles" for their patients!

31 Why did the nurse become a gardener?
To teach patients about the benefits of fresh produce!

32 Why did the doctor start a band?
To use music as therapy for patients!

33 Why did the nurse become a painter?
To create healing and calming artwork for patients' rooms!

34 Why did the doctor become a scientist?
To conduct research for medical advancements!

35 Why did the nurse become a photographer?
To capture special moments of patients' recoveries!

36 Why did the doctor become a veterinarian? To care for animals and keep them healthy!

37 Why did the nurse become a lifeguard? To promote water safety and health!

38 Why did the doctor become an athlete? To encourage patients to stay active and fit!

39 Why did the nurse become a motivational speaker? To inspire patients to stay positive and determined!

40 Why did the doctor become a storyteller? To share medical knowledge through engaging tales!

41 Why did the nurse become a counselor?
To provide emotional support for patients and their families!

42 Why did the doctor become a fashion designer?
To create stylish and comfortable medical attire!

43 Why did the nurse become a pilot?
To deliver medical aid to remote areas!

44 Why did the doctor become a firefighter?
To respond to medical emergencies in any situation!

45 Why did the nurse become a chef?
To create healthy and delicious meals for patients!

46 Why did the doctor become an architect?
To design state-of-the-art medical facilities!

47 Why did the nurse become a scientist?
To study medical breakthroughs and innovations!

48 Why did the doctor become a comedian?
To make patients laugh and brighten their day!

49 Why did the doctor take up gardening?
To learn about plant "medicines"!

50 What did the doctor prescribe for a sick teddy bear?
Plenty of "teddycillin"!

Ghost Jokes

1 What do you call a ghost's mom and dad?
Transparent!

2 Why do ghosts love elevators?
Because it lifts their spirits!

3 What's a ghost's favorite dessert?
I-scream!

4 Why don't ghosts like rain on Halloween?
It dampens their spirits!

5 Where do ghosts go for vacation?
Mali-boo!

 Why did the ghost go to school?
To improve their haunting skills!

7 What do you call a baby ghost?
A little boo-boo!

8 How do you make a tissue dance?
Put a little boo-gie in it!

9 Why did the ghost take up knitting?
It wanted to make boo-tiful blankets!

10 Why did the ghost go to the party?
To have a spooktacular time!

11 What do you get when you cross a ghost with a snowman?
Frostbite!

12 Why don't ghosts like parties?
Because they can't handle the boos!

13 Why are ghosts bad at lying?
Because you can see right through them!

14 What kind of mistakes do ghosts make?
Boo boos!

15 Why did the ghost become a chef?
To learn how to make "ghoul-ash"!

16 How do ghosts keep their hair in place?
With scare spray!

17 What's a ghost's favorite fruit?
Boo-berries!

18 Why don't ghosts ever tell lies?
Because you can see right through them!

19 What do you call a ghost that's always ready to fight?
A "grrrr"-sly ghost!

20 What's a ghost's favorite breakfast?
Ghost toasties!

21 Why did the ghost go to the party?
To have a spooktacular time!

22 What's a ghost's favorite ride at the amusement park?
The roller-ghoster!

23 Why are ghosts such great storytellers?
They have a talent for making things spooky!

24 What do ghosts use to wash their hair?
Shampoo-boo!

25 Why did the ghost become a detective?
To solve "cold cases"!

26 Why did the ghost join the band?
It could play the "spook-tar"!

27 What kind of makeup do ghosts wear?
Mas-scare-a!

28 Why do ghosts like to ride in elevators?
It lifts their spirits!

29 Why do ghosts like to ride in cars?
Because they don't have to worry about "boo-king" a seat!

30 What's a ghost's favorite fruit?
Boo-berries!

31 Why do ghosts love ice cream?
It's "booooo-tiful"!

32 What's a ghost's favorite pie?
Boo-berry pie!

33 What kind of street does a ghost like best?
A dead end!

34 Why did the ghost go to the dance?
To do the boogie-woogie!

35 What do you call a ghost who loves to party?
The "after-life" of the party!

36 Why did the ghost always tell the truth?
Because lying is so un-boo-lievable!

37 Why do ghosts make good cheerleaders?
They have lots of spirit!

38 Why do ghosts like to ride in elevators?
It lifts their spirits!

39 What's a ghost's favorite breakfast?
Ghost toasties!

40 Why don't ghosts ever lie?
Because you can see right through them!

41 Why do ghosts like to ride in cars?
Because they don't have to worry about "boo-king" a seat!

42 What's a ghost's favorite game?
Peek-a-boo!

43 Why do ghosts love the rain?
It's the perfect weather for boo-tiful days!

44 What do ghosts use to wash their hair?
Shampoo-boo!

45 Why did the ghost become a detective?
To solve "cold cases"!

46 Why do ghosts love ice cream?
It's "booooo-tiful"!

47 What kind of makeup do ghosts wear?
Mas-scare-a!

48 Why did the ghost join the band?
It could play the "spook-tar"!

49 Why do ghosts like to ride in elevators?
It lifts their spirits!

50 Why do ghosts like to ride in cars?
Because they don't have to worry about "boo-king" a seat!

Bonus Jokes

Why don't scientists trust atoms?
Because they make up everything!

What do you call fake spaghetti?
An impasta!

Why don't some fish play piano?
You can't tuna fish!

Why did the scarecrow win an award?
Because he was outstanding in his field!

How does a penguin build its house?
Igloos it together!

What do you call a snowman
with a six-pack?
An abdominal snowman!

What did one ocean say to
the other ocean?
Nothing, they just waved!

Why was the math book
sad?
Because it had too many
problems!

How do you organize a
space party?
You planet!

What do you call a dinosaur with
an extensive vocabulary?
A thesaurus!

What did the buffalo say to his son when he left for school?
Bison!

How do you keep a bull from charging?
Take away its credit card!

Why did the turtle refuse to play cards?
Because it got tired of being dealt with!

What did one ocean say to the other ocean?
Nothing, they just waved!

How does a lion greet the other animals in the field?
"Pleased to eat you!"

What's a frog's favorite candy?
Lollihops!

Why did the scarecrow win an award?
Because he was outstanding in his field!

What do you get when you cross a snowman and a vampire?
Frostbite!

Why did the gum cross the road?
Because it was stuck to the chicken's foot!

How do you make a lemon drop?
Just let it fall!

Why don't ants get sick?
Because they have tiny ant-bodies!

Why did the chicken cross the playground?
To get to the other slide!

What do you call fake spaghetti?
An impasta!

Why don't scientists trust atoms?
Because they make up everything!

How does a penguin build its house?
Igloos it together!

What did one ocean say to the other ocean?
Nothing, they just waved!

How does a lion greet the other animals in the field?
"Pleased to eat you!"

What do you get when you cross a snowman and a vampire?
Frostbite!

What did the buffalo say to his son when he left for school?
Bison!

How do you keep a bull from charging?
Take away its credit card!

Thank you

We wanted to take a moment to express our deepest gratitude for your recent purchase of our books written by our beloved author of kids' stories. Your support and appreciation mean the world to us and serve as a heartwarming affirmation of the hard work and passion that goes into creating these magical tales.

Every word, every character, and every adventure within those pages were crafted with the intention of sparking imaginations, igniting curiosity, and nurturing a love for reading in young minds. It brings us immense joy to know that our stories have found a place in the hearts and homes of children across the world.

We hope that the books you purchased bring endless smiles, laughter, and cherished moments shared between parents and their children. We would be honored if you would consider sharing your thoughts and experiences with us. Your feedback not only helps us improve but also serves as a source of motivation to create more captivating stories in the future.

www.ingramcontent.com/pod-product-compliance
Lightning Source LLC
Chambersburg PA
CBHW071320080526
44587CB00018B/3298